9/95

THUNDERBOLT

THUNDERBOLT

LEARNING ABOUT LIGHTNING

by Jonathan D. Kahl

Lerner Publications Company / Minneapolis

To Carol, with true love

All words printed in **bold** are explained in the glossary that begins on page 51.

A metric conversion chart appears on page 55.

Library of Congress Cataloging-in-Publication Data

Kahl, Jonathan D.
   Thunderbolt : learning about lightning / by Jonathan D. Kahl.
      p.   cm.–(How's the weather?)
   Includes index.
   Summary: Examines what happens in a thunderstorm and how lightning is formed and provides information on the study of lightning, safety measures, and the damage it can cause.
   ISBN 0-8225-2528-3
   1. Lightning–Juvenile literature. [1. Lightning. 2. Thunderstorms.] I. Title. II. Series: Kahl, Jonathan D. How's the weather?
QC966.5.K34 1993
551.5'632–dc20   92-45177
                                                                          CIP
                                                                           AC

Manufactured in the United States of America

1 2 3 4 5 6 – P/JR – 98 97 96 95 94 93

CONTENTS

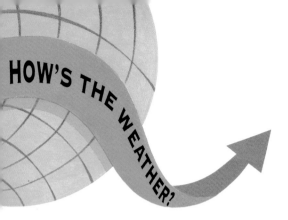

INTRODUCTION

Nature has many different qualities. Sometimes nature is gentle and pleasant. Other times it is violent and fierce. Some of the most violent natural events, like landslides, tidal waves, tornadoes, and hurricanes, are uncommon occurrences that most people never see during their lifetimes. There is one natural phenomenon, though, that is both powerful and common: lightning.

Lightning is a massive spark of **electricity** created inside a **cumulonimbus cloud**. Another name for a cumulonimbus cloud is a thunderstorm. Thunder is the booming or rumbling sound that accompanies a lightning flash.

Lightning can travel between two cumulonimbus clouds, between two parts of the same cloud, or from a cloud to the ground. When lightning hits the ground, it tends to strike tall, isolated objects like buildings and trees.

A lightning flash carries an electrical **charge** of about 100 million volts—a million times greater than the charge running through the wires in your house. Lightning heats the air to more than 54,000° Fahrenheit—five times hotter than the surface of the Sun!

A hiker inspects a tree trunk split by lightning.

Lightning is capable of killing people and animals, splitting tree trunks, and starting fires. Lightning strikes cause more than 10,000 forest fires in the United States each year. Lightning isn't just a destructive force on Earth though. Scientists believe that lightning helps form nitrogen oxides, chemicals that enrich the soil and help plants grow. In this way, lightning plays an important role in the creation of life on Earth.

Lightning strikes Tucson, Arizona, at sunset.

Meteorologists, scientists who study the weather, want to learn more about lightning. They use sophisticated instruments and computers to predict thunderstorms and track lightning damage. Scientists even create lightning flashes in laboratories.

In this book, you will learn how thunderstorms create electricity, how lightning travels through the sky, and how scientists study lightning. You'll also learn about the weather conditions that bring thunder and lightning, and you'll find out how to protect yourself from a lightning strike.

ELECTRIC POWER

Lamps, telephones, radios, washing machines, and other household appliances all run on electric power. Electricity is used to operate industrial machines and to start motor vehicles. Satellites, computers, and televisions are some of the many important communication devices that run on electricity.

A lightning flash carries a tremendous electrical charge—enough to light an entire city. But because a lightning flash occurs within a fraction of a second, and because lightning strikes are unpredictable, the electricity from lightning isn't usable in homes or industry. Instead, people get electric power from batteries and generators.

1

ELECTRICAL STORMS

To learn about lightning, we must first learn about thunderstorms, the clouds that create lightning. A thunderstorm goes through three stages during its life: the *cumulus*, *mature*, and *dissipating* stages. The entire process typically takes about two hours.

The Thunderstorm Life Cycle

Thunderstorms usually form in spring and summer—late in the afternoon, when temperatures have reached their highest levels for the day. The cumulus stage begins when the Sun's rays heat the air near the ground. The hot air rises.

The hot, rising air contains **water vapor**—water that has been **evaporated**, or turned into an invisible gas by the heat of the Sun. The currents of rising air cool as they reach higher altitudes, where the atmosphere is colder. Water vapor in the air cools and **condenses**, turning from gas back into tiny liquid water droplets. The water droplets gather together in the sky, forming a **cumulus cloud**—a puffy, white cloud that resembles a big ball of cotton.

As water vapor condenses, it gives off a special kind of energy called **latent heat**. Latent heat warms the air inside the cloud once more, and the cloud rises higher into the sky.

A cloud containing a lot of water vapor gives off a lot of latent heat. The cloud grows taller and taller—sometimes as tall as six miles—and becomes a cumulonimbus cloud, or thunderstorm.

Currents of rising air, called **updrafts**, carry small water droplets and ice crystals upward through the cloud. The droplets bump into one another, combine, and become larger and heavier. When the droplets become too heavy to remain suspended in the

A cumulonimbus cloud begins to grow over the Wyoming plains.

air, they fall to the ground as rain. Rainfall, along with thunder and lightning, marks the mature stage of the thunderstorm.

Falling raindrops pull some air down with them, creating downward-moving air currents, or **downdrafts**. As rainfall becomes stronger, downdrafts grow stronger too. Before long the downdrafts become stronger than the updrafts in a thunderstorm, and the storm begins the dissipating, or dissolving, stage. Rainfall becomes lighter and eventually stops. The giant cumulonimbus cloud evaporates and disappears.

Thunderstorms are a common occurrence in almost everyone's life.

Electrical Charges

Thunderstorms are called electrical storms because they produce a type of energy called electricity. To understand how thunderstorms create electricity, we must first know something about **atoms**.

Atoms are the basic units of matter. Every substance, including air and water, is made up of atoms. Atoms are too small to be seen using an ordinary microscope. An atom is more than a million times smaller than the width of a human hair.

An atom has two parts: a nucleus (or center), containing particles called **protons** and **neutrons**, and an orbit (outer rings), containing particles called **electrons**. Protons and electrons are attracted to each other like metal to a magnet. This attraction causes electrons to circle the nucleus of an atom in the same way that the Moon orbits the Earth.

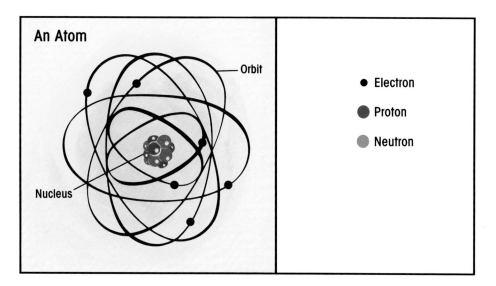

An Atom

Orbit

Nucleus

● Electron

● Proton

● Neutron

The term *charge* is used to describe a buildup of electrical energy. Protons carry a positive electrical charge and electrons carry a negative electrical charge. (Neutrons have no electrical charge.) Positive and negative charges are always attracted to each other.

Atoms usually carry the same number of protons and electrons. The positive and negative charges inside an atom balance one another, so most atoms are electrically neutral.

But, since atoms are always moving around and bumping into one another, electrons sometimes break away from their orbits and begin orbiting nearby atoms. An atom that gains extra electrons will carry a negative charge. An atom that loses electrons will carry a positive charge.

Since positive and negative charges are attracted to one another, electrons in a negatively charged atom will try to move toward a positively charged atom. This movement of electrons is called an electrical **discharge**. Sparks and lightning are two kinds of electrical discharges.

Electrical charges are generated inside a thunderstorm by updrafts and downdrafts, which carry water and ice crystals through the cloud. When objects collide inside a thunderstorm—like water droplets hitting ice crystals or hailstones—electrons jump from one atom to another.

Warmer, heavier objects—like raindrops and hailstones—tend to gain electrons during the collisions. These objects settle to the bottom of the cloud, creating a negative charge there. Colder, lighter particles—like ice crystals and slivers broken off from hailstones—tend to lose electrons in the collisions. The lighter

Electricity flows easily through metal power lines and telephone cables.

particles rise to the top of the cloud, giving this region a positive charge. With different electrical charges in different parts of a thunderstorm, the stage is set for an electrical discharge.

Before describing a lightning flash itself, we must first examine an important scientific property: **conductivity**. Conductivity refers to the ability of a substance to carry electricity. Electricity flows more easily through some materials than through others.

Metal is a good conductor of electricity—that's why utility wires are made of metal. Water is also a good electrical conductor.

CREATE YOUR OWN LIGHTNING

In a dark room, rub a plastic comb against a piece of dry wool or fur. Hold the comb near a metal doorknob. You should see a small spark.

By rubbing the comb, you cause the buildup of negative electrical charges, which are attracted to positive charges on the doorknob. The spark you see is a discharge of electricity as electrons flow between positive and negative charges.

◄ Lightning explodes from a towering thunderstorm.

Therefore, you should never use electric appliances near a bathtub, swimming pool, or standing water. You risk electrical shock, or even death, should the current travel through water to your body.

Air, on the other hand, is a poor conductor of electricity. Electricity will not normally flow through air unless electrical charges are extremely strong. When electrical charges within a thunderstorm become strong enough to overpower the weak conductivity of air, the charges explode as a massive electrical discharge—a lightning flash.

FULGURITES

Fulgurites, sometimes called petrified lightning, are created when lightning strikes sand. The high temperatures melt the sand, which eventually cools and hardens into a crusty tube of glass. Fulgurites sometimes resemble the roots of a tree. The next time you're at the beach, clear away some sand and see if you can find any fulgurites.

The largest fulgurite ever found was discovered in South Amboy, New Jersey. This piece of petrified lightning is 9 feet long and 3 inches across at its widest point. A beautiful 4½-foot-long fulgurite is on display at the Academy of Natural Sciences in Philadelphia.

Thunder

Air expands when it's heated. That is, the molecules, or particles, of air spread out. Air contracts, or shrinks, when it's cooled. Blow up a balloon and put it in the refrigerator for a few minutes. The balloon shrinks as the air cools. When you remove the balloon from the refrigerator, the air inside the balloon warms quickly. The air expands and the balloon expands too.

A lightning flash heats the air to 54,000°F in less than 1/5 of a second. The heating is so intense and sudden that the air molecules near a lightning flash actually explode—creating waves of energy known as "shock waves". A shock wave, which is a kind of sound wave, is also called thunder.

SOUND WAVES

Sound waves are produced by vibrations. When we speak, air vibrates against our vocal cords. Instruments create musical sounds with vibrating strings, reeds, or drumheads.

Thunder is created by vibrations too. Hot air exploding away from a lightning flash collides with colder air nearby. The air vibrates, creating a sound we call thunder.

Thunder from a distant electrical storm might echo off mountains and hills, creating a rumbling sound.

Every lightning flash produces thunder. If you are close to a lightning flash, the thunder may sound like a loud crash. A flash with many branches often produces a crackling sound. If you are far away from a lightning flash, the thunder might sound like a deep rumble. The rumbling is caused by sound waves from different parts of the lightning flash reaching your ears at different times. The sounds merge and create a rumbling noise.

Sound travels at about 1,100 feet (1/5 mile) per second. Suppose a thunderstorm were passing overhead, and lightning struck a mile away from you. The sound of thunder would take five seconds to travel the distance of one mile from the lightning flash to your ears. Light, however, travels at the amazing speed of 186,000 miles per second. The light of the flash would reach your eyes in about one-millionth of a second—almost instantly.

Lightning is beautiful. But remember, it's also deadly!

You can use this knowledge to compute your distance from a lightning strike. Simply count the number of seconds between the sight of the lightning flash and the sound of the thunder. Divide the number by five and you'll know how many miles stand between you and the lightning. If you hear thunder nearly at the same time you see lightning, the stroke is very near, and you should seek shelter immediately.

INSIDE A THUNDERSTORM

Updrafts and downdrafts, moving at speeds of up to 100 miles per hour, carry water and ice crystals up and down inside thunderstorms. At the top of the cloud— where temperatures can be as low as – 40°F—raindrops often freeze into solid balls of ice. Sometimes the balls of ice are carried up and down several times until they finally fall from the cloud as hailstones.

►This towering cumulus cloud will soon be a cumulonimbus cloud. Cumulonimbus clouds can grow to be six miles high!

►Hailstones litter a field of wildflowers after a thunderstorm.

Thunderstorm Weather

Every day about 44,000 thunderstorms develop on Earth. A single thunderstorm can produce hundreds of lightning flashes, and lightning strikes the Earth millions of times each day.

Even on this clear summer day in Florida, a thunderstorm might be in the forecast.

Most of the world's thunderstorms occur in the tropics—a hot, humid region near the equator. The equator is also the meeting place of two powerful wind systems, the northeast and southeast trade winds. As the trade winds collide near the equator, the air in the center of the collision piles up and rises. The hot, rising air—which is rich in water vapor—produces frequent thunderstorms.

Thunderstorms and lightning are also common in the southeastern United States. There, warm, humid air from the Gulf of Mexico meets cool, dry air from Canada. The places where warm and cold air meet are called **fronts**. Warm air rises above cold air at a front, water vapor cools and condenses, and thunderstorms often form.

Thunderstorms visit the southeastern United States between 70 and 100 days a year. The most lightning-prone area of the United States is southern Florida. Every square mile of land in this region is struck by lightning about 40 times a year.

2

LIGHTNING FLASHES

About 100 years ago, scientists began to use high-speed photography to study lightning. Photographs revealed that a lightning flash is actually composed of several distinct electrical discharges, or strokes.

A typical lightning flash occurs in less than 1/5 of a second and contains 10 to 15 individual strokes. The electricity within each stroke moves at the astonishing speed of 31,000 miles per second. The human eye is not quick enough to identify these individual strokes. To us, the sequence of discharges looks like one bright, flickering flash.

Anatomy of a Lightning Flash

As we have learned, electricity travels between negative and positive electrical charges. Lightning can travel between negative and positive regions in two different clouds (*cloud-to-cloud lightning*) or between negative and positive regions within the same cloud (*intracloud lightning*). Intracloud lightning accounts for most of the lightning—60 percent—produced during a thunderstorm.

Some lightning—like these intracloud flashes over Miami—doesn't travel to the ground.

The form of lightning people are most familiar with, though, is *cloud-to-ground lightning*. As charges build inside a thunderstorm, the ground below the cloud becomes electrically charged too. Positive charges, attracted by the strong negative charges at the base of a thunderstorm, build up on tall objects on the ground such as trees, flagpoles, and buildings. Cloud-to-ground lightning results from this attraction.

First, electrons at the base of a thunderstorm stream from the cloud toward the ground in a series of steps. This series is called a **stepped leader**. The electrons take a branching path to Earth, moving downward between 60 and 300 feet in each step. The stepped leader doesn't produce much light, and we can barely see it.

HOW TO PHOTOGRAPH LIGHTNING

You can easily and safely photograph lightning using an automatic 35-millimeter camera with a feature called "aperture priority." Wait until dark and follow these steps:

1. Place your camera on a steady surface, such as a flat table or a tripod. Do not hold the camera.

2. Point the camera toward a distant thunderstorm, making sure there are no other sources of light (streetlights, headlights, etc.) between the camera and the storm.

3. Adjust the aperture to the highest possible setting (usually F-22). This setting reduces the lens opening, allowing less light to come into the camera.

4. Release the shutter. Your automatic camera will take a photograph with a very long exposure (several seconds). If lightning occurs within this period, the flash will be recorded on film. You can usually get a good lightning photo after only a few exposures.

Positive electrical charges on the ground are attracted to negative charges at the base of a thunderstorm cloud. The positive charges cluster around tall objects, like flagpoles.

When the stepped leader comes within about 300 feet of the ground, the electrons draw a positive charge from the ground into the air. This charge is called an **upward streamer**. Once the upward streamer meets the stepped leader, electricity flows through the entire channel, creating a bright flash between the cloud and the ground. This flash, called a **return stroke**, is as bright as a million 100-watt light bulbs.

Then, more electrons flow from the cloud, usually taking the same path to Earth as did the stepped leader. This second discharge of electrons, called a **dart leader**, is met near the ground by another upward streamer. The meeting is followed by another return stroke.

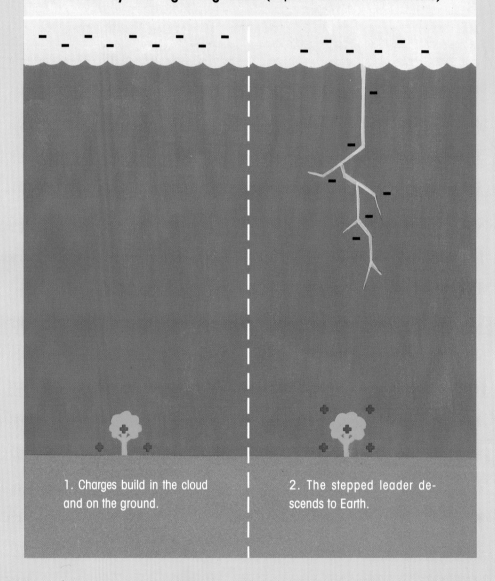

Anatomy of a Lightning Flash (sequence takes less than ⅕ second)

1. Charges build in the cloud and on the ground.

2. The stepped leader descends to Earth.

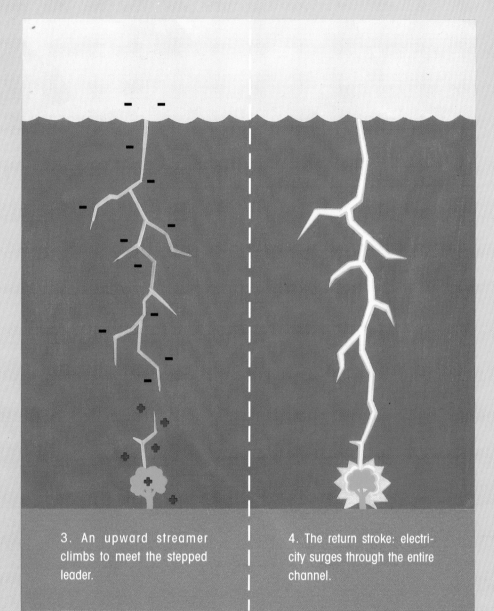

3. An upward streamer climbs to meet the stepped leader.

4. The return stroke: electricity surges through the entire channel.

The sequence of dart leaders and return strokes is repeated several times—usually three or four. Often the entire sequence follows the same path between the cloud and the ground, producing what looks like a single lightning flash. Sometimes, though, the dart leaders and return strokes take different paths through the sky—producing a *forked lightning* flash that strikes the ground in several places.

Types of Lightning

Forked lightning is a common sight during thunderstorms. But lightning can have many different appearances. *Ribbon lightning* occurs when strong winds move individual strokes within a lightning flash, creating a narrow ribbon of light. *Sheet lightning* appears when clouds block our view of a lightning flash, creating a glowing white light in the sky. *Bead lightning,* created when parts of a lightning flash start to fade, looks like a series of bright beads or pearls in the sky.

Lightning from a distant thunderstorm is often called *heat lightning.* Heat lightning looks like a flickering cloud in the distance. People sometimes think that heat lightning is a special kind of lightning, because we see it but don't hear any thunder. Actually, all lightning is accompanied by thunder. Heat lightning just occurs so far away that the sound doesn't reach our ears.

Perhaps the most peculiar form of lightning is *ball lightning*—also known as a fireball or lightning ball. This mysterious phenomenon looks like a bright red or yellow ball of light that appears to float in the air or dart about wildly. Lightning balls are usually between 4 and 16 inches across and generally fly around for a second or two before quietly fizzling out or exploding with a loud bang.

It's easy to see how forked lightning got its name.

Sheet lightning creates an eerie glow in the sky.

Nobody knows what causes ball lightning. Several scientists have attempted to create ball lightning in the laboratory, but so far these efforts have been unsuccessful. Despite more than 1,600 observations reported during the past 150 years, ball lightning remains one of the greatest mysteries of thunderstorm and lightning activity.

Ribbon lightning (top); a lightning flash inside a double rainbow (bottom)

3

LIGHTNING AND PEOPLE

People have feared and respected thunder and lightning for thousands of years. Ancient people understood very little about the weather; they thought lightning was a weapon of the gods. In ancient Greece, Zeus, the king of the gods, was said to use lightning to punish the wicked.

Of the many ancient gods associated with lightning, none is more famous than Thor, the fierce redheaded god of the Norse people. According to Norse mythology, Thor rode across the sky in a chariot and produced lightning with a magic hammer. Although an ancient story, the legend of Thor lives to this day. The word Thursday means "Thor's day." The German word for Thursday is *Donnerstag*, which means "thunder day."

During the Middle Ages, many people thought they could repel lightning by ringing church bells. In fact, many medieval church bells bear the Latin inscription *"Fulgura Frango,"* which means "I break up the lightning flashes."

Since lightning tends to strike tall, isolated objects, church towers have been frequent targets for lightning strikes. During the

Thor fights off giants with his magic hammer.

1700s, lightning struck more than 375 churches in Europe, killing at least 100 bell ringers. To make matters worse, people sometimes stored gunpowder and weapons in churches. A lightning strike in 1769 at a church in Brescia, Italy, ignited 100 tons of gunpowder, causing an explosion that killed 3,000 people.

Studying Lightning

One of the first people to study lightning was the early American leader Benjamin Franklin. Franklin was a scientist with a keen interest in the weather. He long suspected that lightning was a form of electricity.

Although scientists knew very little about electricity in Franklin's day, they understood that electricity could travel through metal wire and cause a spark. If lightning was electricity, Franklin reasoned, then it too would travel through a metal wire.

Benjamin Franklin made some of the earliest and most important contributions to lightning research.

In 1752 Franklin proved his theory by performing a simple (but dangerous) experiment. Franklin flew an ordinary kite during a thunderstorm. But instead of using string, Franklin flew his kite on a metal wire. He tied a short piece of silk string to the bottom of the wire, along with a metal key, and held the string in his hand.

As the kite flew, electricity from the thunderstorm traveled through the wire to the string in Franklin's hand. Since electricity cannot travel through silk, the electric current "jumped" from the wire to the metal key, creating a spark. This famous spark was actually a miniature lightning flash. (Never try to repeat Franklin's experiment yourself. The results could be deadly.)

Benjamin Franklin's study of lightning did not stop with this experiment. Franklin also invented a device to protect buildings from lightning damage. The "Franklin Rod," now called a lightning rod, is a long metal bar with a pointed tip.

A lightning rod attaches to a building, with the tip of the rod extending well above the building's roof. Since lightning tends to strike the tallest object in an area, the rod—not the building—will usually take a lightning strike. The powerful electrical charge then travels from the rod, through a heavy wire alongside the building, to a metal spike buried in the ground. The building is spared any damage—such as fire—that lightning could cause. Today, nearly every tall building, tower, and ship has a lightning rod.

The invention of photography in the late 1800s helped scientists learn more about lightning. Scientists were able to analyze photographs of lightning like individual frames of a movie. In this way, they discovered that a lightning flash was actually a series of several electrical discharges.

ROCKET-INDUCED LIGHTNING

To learn about lightning, scientists launch small metal rockets beneath cumulonimbus clouds. These rockets act like flying lightning rods and instantly draw a lightning strike. The lightning travels along a wire to a machine that measures the discharge.

►Rocket-induced lightning strikes—next to the trail of smoke left by the rocket.

The 20th century has brought significant advances in meteorology. Scientists study the weather using radar systems, satellite photography, weather balloons, computers, and special airplanes designed to fly right through thunderstorms.

For many years, human observers working at weather stations tracked lightning strokes and recorded them by hand. Recently, scientists have developed instruments called lightning sensors that automatically record electrical discharges in the atmosphere. Using lightning sensors and computers, weather forecasters have set up a network called the Lightning Protection and Tracking System. The system monitors lightning strikes around the clock.

Scientists set up a lightning sensor in Australia.

A miniature lightning flash created in the lab

Meteorologists use the system to track the movement of electrical storms and to improve thunderstorm forecasts. Forest rangers also want to know about lightning activity so they can predict where forest fires might start. Electric utility companies worry about lightning strikes, which can destroy telephone and power lines. Finally, the tracking system helps airplane pilots avoid thunderstorms.

Lightning Damage

Lightning is extremely hazardous to both property and people. The heat from a lightning flash can evaporate water instantly and melt metal. Trees, brick walls, and other objects sometimes even explode when lightning strikes them. Just the shock wave from a nearby lightning flash is powerful enough to knock you off your feet.

Lightning is responsible for thousands of forest fires each year.

Each year lightning causes nearly $100 million in property damage in the United States alone. Lightning is the major cause of forest fires on Earth, igniting thousands of fires and destroying more than $50 million in timber every year.

Lightning frequently hits airplanes—often damaging sensitive navigation equipment, temporarily blinding pilots, and disrupting radio communications. More than once, an aircraft has crashed to the ground, killing pilots and passengers, after lightning damaged the plane's mechanical equipment.

Spacecraft on a launch pad, because they project high into the air, frequently act like giant lightning rods. On March 26, 1987, an Atlas-Centaur rocket and a U.S. Navy satellite, together worth $161 million, were destroyed by lightning at Cape Canaveral, Florida. Scientists are working hard to develop surge protectors that will prevent lightning damage to rockets, airplanes, and other vehicles.

In the United States alone, lightning kills about 100 people each year and injures several hundred more. On average, lightning kills more people per year than floods, hurricanes, tornadoes, and other weather disasters combined.

Two out of every three people struck by lightning fully recover. Usually, survivors are not struck by lightning directly; most are injured when electricity jumps from a nearby object, such as a tree, into their bodies. Lightning victims frequently lose consciousness, and many require treatment for shock or burns.

Few people who suffer a *direct* lightning strike will survive. A direct hit can damage vital organs and stop a person's heart. Most lightning deaths result from heart attacks.

The Empire State Building in New York City is struck by lightning more than 20 times each year. On one occasion, the building was hit 15 times in 15 minutes!

Your chances of being struck by lightning are slim—about 350,000 to 1. However, one unlucky park ranger, Roy Sullivan (nicknamed "the Lightning Conductor of Virginia"), was struck by lightning seven times! He lost his big toenail to lightning in 1942 and his eyebrows in 1969. His hair caught on fire twice and he suffered burns during the strikes.

Lightning Safety

One of the most important things you can learn about lightning is how to protect yourself from it. Even though lightning is fascinating and beautiful to watch, you must never forget that it is also powerful and deadly.

The best way to protect yourself from lightning is to stay indoors during thunderstorms. Don't wait until a storm is underway before seeking shelter. Lightning might strike even before rain falls from a thunderstorm.

When inside, keep away from metal pipes, wires, and faucets, which may conduct electricity. Don't talk on the telephone. Many people have been killed when lightning traveled through utility wires to the telephone in their hands.

Golfers are particularly at risk for lightning strikes because golf courses are usually open fields with a number of isolated trees. Golfers also carry metal clubs, which might attract lightning.

If you are not near a building during a thunderstorm, take shelter in a car or a truck with a metal roof. When lightning strikes the roof of a car, electricity travels through the metal and jumps safely to the ground without injuring the passengers. The bed of a pickup truck or a car with a convertible cloth top will not provide protection from lightning, however.

People who spend time outdoors should learn the rules of lightning safety.

If you are caught outside in a thunderstorm and cannot find a car or building, look for a natural shelter such as a cliff, cave, valley, or dry ditch. Do not stand under a lone tree, which is likely to attract lightning.

Certain warning signs might alert you that lightning is about to strike nearby. Metal objects might start to buzz or crackle. These sounds are caused by a buildup of positive electrical charges on the ground. If your skin begins to tingle or your hair stands on end during a storm, electrical charges might be building up on *you*. Crouch down (do not lie down) immediately until the warning signs pass. If you stand up, you may become a lightning rod!

Remember that lightning tends to strike tall, isolated objects and that water is a good electrical conductor. With these facts in mind, you can protect yourself and your companions from lightning by observing the following guidelines during thunderstorms:

- Stay clear of objects that stand out above their surroundings, such as isolated trees, flagpoles, telephone poles, hills, and rooftops.
- Stay away from bodies of water, such as lakes and swimming pools.
- Do not touch metal objects like wire fences, railroad tracks, golf clubs, aluminum baseball bats, bicycles, or umbrellas.
- If you are on open ground, crouch down, keep your head as low as possible, and touch the ground only with your feet. Do not lie down. Electrical current from a nearby lightning strike may travel toward you along wet ground.
- When indoors, stay away from appliances, metal pipes, and wires.

A triple-branch flash strikes the Earth.

If someone near you is struck by lightning, don't be afraid to touch the person. Lightning victims carry no electrical charge and may be handled without any risk of electric shock. Lightning victims who are not breathing may be revived by mouth-to-mouth resuscitation or CPR (cardiopulmonary resuscitation). Do not attempt to treat a lightning victim yourself, however, unless you have been trained in first aid. Call a fire, police, or emergency medical crew immediately.

By now, you've learned some interesting facts about thunder and lightning. The most important fact to remember is that lightning is a powerful force of nature that should always be respected and feared. With this in mind, you can safely appreciate the awesome beauty of this common weather event. Benjamin Franklin once said: "Some people are weatherwise, but most are otherwise." Isn't it nice to be one of the few?

GLOSSARY

atoms: the most basic units of matter. All substances are made up of atoms.

charge: a buildup of electrical energy caused by the movement of electrons. Something that has gained electrons carries a negative charge. Something that has lost electrons carries a positive charge.

condense: to turn from a gas into a liquid by cooling

conductivity: the ability of a substance to conduct, or carry, an electric current

cumulonimbus cloud: a large cloud that brings lightning, rain, hail, and strong winds. Another name for a cumulonimbus cloud is a thunderstorm.

cumulus cloud: a puffy, white cloud, commonly seen on summer afternoons. Cumulus clouds sometimes grow into cumulonimbus clouds.

dart leader: a discharge of electrons that follows a return stroke of a lightning flash

discharge: the movement of electrons between negative and positive charges

downdrafts: downward-moving air currents found inside thunderstorms

electricity: a form of energy used to provide heat, light, and power

electrons: particles inside atoms that carry a negative charge

evaporate: to turn from a liquid into a gas by heating

front: the boundary between a mass of warm air and a mass of cold air. Thunderstorms often form at fronts.

latent heat: a special kind of energy released when water vapor condenses

meteorologists: the scientists who study and predict the weather

neutrons: particles inside atoms that carry no electrical charge

protons: particles inside atoms that carry a positive electrical charge

return stroke: a visible lightning flash. A return stroke is created when an upward streamer meets a stepped leader.

stepped leader: the discharge of electrons that precedes a lightning flash

updrafts: upward-moving air currents, often found inside thunderstorms

upward streamer: an electrical discharge that rises from the ground to meet a stepped leader

water vapor: water in gas form

Opposite: At an amusement park in Wisconsin, visitors find out what happens when electrical charges build up on a person's body. The exhibit is safe. But if you are outside and your hair stands on end, you might be in danger of a lightning strike. Crouch down immediately!

Hair Raising Experience

INDEX

METRIC CONVERSION CHART		
When you know:	multiply by:	to find:
acres	.41	hectares
square miles	2.59	square kilometers
gallons	3.79	liters
inches	2.54	centimeters
feet	.30	meters
yards	.91	meters
miles	1.61	kilometers
pounds	.45	kilograms
tons	.91	metric tons
degrees Fahrenheit	.56 (after subtracting 32)	degrees Celsius

ACKNOWLEDGMENTS

Photographs and illustrations reproduced with permission of Johnny Autery, p. 2; © Scott T. Smith, p. 7; Kent Wood, pp. 8, 16, 17, 19, 20, 21 (top), 31, 33 (top), 47, 48, 50; Northern States Power, pp. 9, 15; Martin G. Kleinsorge, p. 11; Jeff Greenberg, p. 12; Liz Monson, pp. 13, 28, 29; British Tourist Authority, p. 18; Jo-Ann Ordano, p. 21 (bottom); Robert Czarnomski, p. 22; © David Molchos, pp. 25, 56; Bill Marchel, pp. 26, 32, 41; Daphne Kinzler, p. 27; David A. Ponton, p. 33 (bottom); National Museum, Stockholm, p. 35; Metropolitan Museum of Art, p. 36; Earle Williams, MIT, pp. 38, 39, 40; New York State Department of Economic Development, p. 43; PGA of America/Steven J. Gilbert, p. 44; Marybeth Lorbiecki, p. 45; Wisconsin Dells Visitor and Convention Bureau, p. 53. Cover photograph by Kent Wood.